When It Rains

Written by Rose Kelbrick • Illustrated by Denise Durkin

When it rains,
Dad comes inside.

2

When it rains,
Mom comes inside.

When it rains,
my brother comes inside.

7

When it rains,
the dog comes inside.

8

9

When it rains,
the cat comes inside.

10

When it rains,
I go outside.

13

15